T0005522

Let
Us
March
On!

Let Us March On!

James Weldon Johnson
and the
Silent Protest Parade

by Yohuru Williams and Michael G. Long

art by Xia Gordon

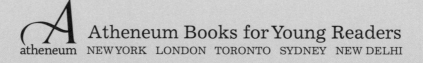

Atheneum Books for Young Readers
atheneum NEW YORK LONDON TORONTO SYDNEY NEW DELHI

ACKNOWLEDGMENTS

Our wonderful editor, Reka Simonsen, deserves our
deepest gratitude for her enthusiasm and excellence.
We're also grateful for the rest of the awesome team at Atheneum.

Our gratitude extends to our wise and exceptional agents, Joan Brookbank
and John Rudolph, for their support and encouragement.

Yohuru thanks his mom, Elizabeth Williams, for instilling his love of
children's literature, and his partner and favorite elementary teacher,
Alexandra Alves, for rekindling that passion.

Mike thanks his family—Karin, Jackson, Elda, and Nate—for all their cheers.

With appreciation beyond words, we remember the hundreds of silent
protesters, especially the children, who dared to march against racial violence
in 1917. Their courageous witness remains breathtaking.

ATHENEUM BOOKS FOR YOUNG READERS

An imprint of Simon & Schuster Children's Publishing Division

1230 Avenue of the Americas, New York, New York 10020

Text © 2024 by Yohuru Williams and Michael G. Long

Illustration © 2024 by Xia Gordon

Book design by Greg Stadnyk © 2024 by Simon & Schuster, LLC

All rights reserved, including the right of reproduction in whole or in part in any form.

ATHENEUM BOOKS FOR YOUNG READERS is a registered trademark of Simon & Schuster, LLC.

Atheneum logo is a trademark of Simon & Schuster, LLC.

Simon & Schuster: Celebrating 100 Years of Publishing in 2024

For information about special discounts for bulk purchases, please contact

Simon & Schuster Special Sales at 1-866-506-1949 or business@simonandschuster.com.

The Simon & Schuster Speakers Bureau can bring authors to your live event.

For more information or to book an event, contact the Simon & Schuster Speakers Bureau at

1-866-248-3049 or visit our website at www.simonspeakers.com.

The text for this book was set in Excelsior.

The illustrations for this book were rendered digitally.

Manufactured in China

0124 SCP

First Edition

2 4 6 8 10 9 7 5 3 1

CIP data for this book is available from the Library of Congress.

ISBN 9781665902786

ISBN 9781665902793 (ebook)

To all the silent children who deep down cry out for peace and justice
—Y. W. and M. G. L.

To Mom, Dad, and Ché for loving and leading me to a place you always knew I'd find
—X. G.

When James Weldon Johnson spoke,
people listened,
silently,
making sure they heard everything.

James was a man of words—
a brilliant lawyer, an inspiring teacher,
and a distinguished poet.

He had once penned a poem
so uplifting, so inspiring, and so beautiful
that people called it "the Black national anthem."

Lift every voice and sing
Till earth and heaven ring,
Ring with the harmonies of Liberty . . .

People often turned to James for advice
in troubling times.
As a man of words, he knew what to say.
And now was one of those times.

White people had long hurt Black people,
but in recent days, violent attacks had increased
in scary and shocking ways.

James decided to hold a meeting and make a plan.
When it was his turn to speak, everyone leaned forward,
silently,
expectantly.

James cleared his throat.
"I have an idea," he said.

"Let us march," he said,
"in New York City."

A big protest
on the biggest avenue
in the biggest city
in the country.

"And," he said,
slowly and quietly,
"let's make it a silent march."

No chanting.
No cheering.
No chuckling.

Just serious,
somber
silence.

"You know me as a man of words,"
James explained.
"But sometimes silence can be more powerful
and attract more attention
than yelling and screaming and shouting.

"I believe that our silence will show others
how much we hurt,
and how strong and serious we are."

Then James waited,
silently,
expectantly,
hopefully.

Finally the room . . .

ERUPTED!

"YES!"

"LET'S DO IT!"

As James felt the room
shaking with excitement,
he saw several children
already practicing their march steps.

Facing the rising sun of our new day begun,
Let us march on till victory is won.

James and his coleaders worked hard
throughout the next week.
They mapped a parade route down Fifth Avenue.
They asked government officials
for permission to protest.

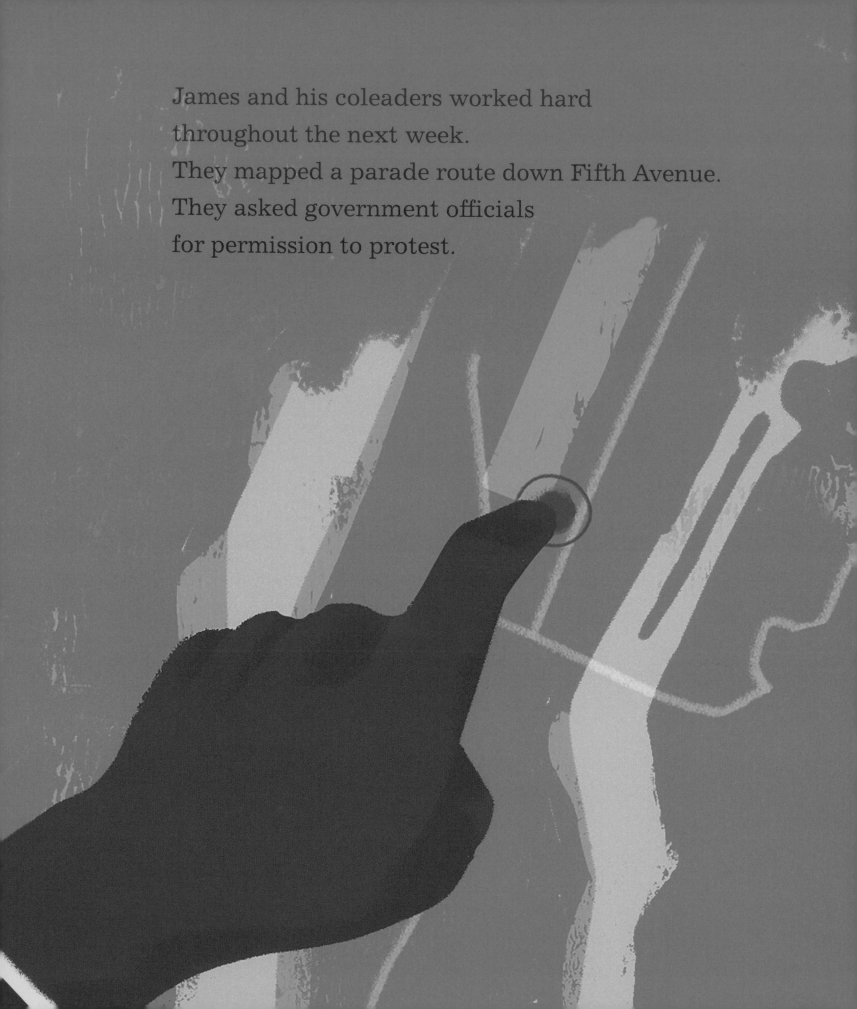

They wrote flyers explaining the purpose
of the march.
They enlisted nurses to take care of anyone
who might become sick.
They dotted every *i* and crossed every *t*
as they prepared for the big day.

The day of the march was terribly hot and humid,
but James noticed a slight breeze
as he walked to the corner of Fifth Avenue and Fifty-Ninth Street,
where the march would begin.

As James approached the corner,
he couldn't believe what he saw.

Ten thousand people were ready to march!
A stern-looking man barked out orders:

"At one p.m. *SHARP*,
start marching down Fifth Avenue,
and *KEEP QUIET*!
This is a *SILENT* march!"

James helped to lead the march.
As a man of words,
he felt an urge to speak
every now and then.
But even he kept silent.

The only sound came from
quietly beating drums
that kept everyone in step.

The silence was so stunning,
so strong and powerful,
that everyone felt the importance
of the march deep in their hearts.

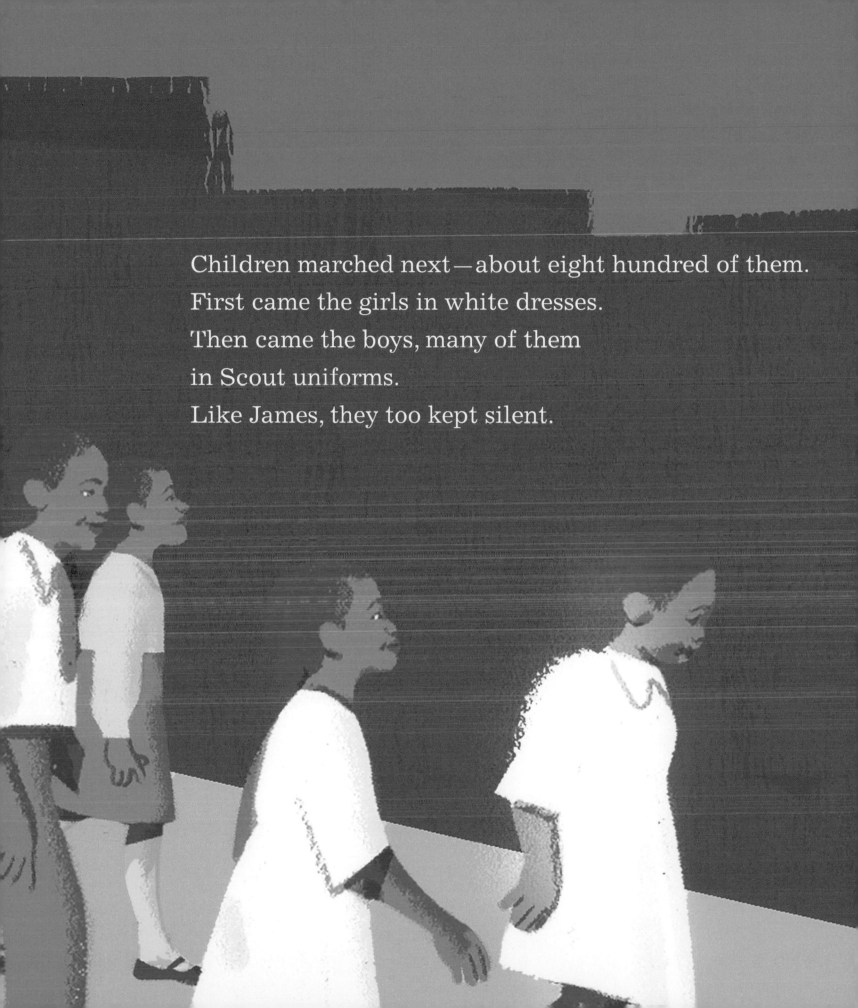

Children marched next—about eight hundred of them.
First came the girls in white dresses.
Then came the boys, many of them
in Scout uniforms.
Like James, they too kept silent.

Finally came the adults.
Women first, then men.
Rather than saying anything,
they carried signs with messages about equality, fairness,
and the contributions that Black people had made
to the United States.

One sign referred to Crispus Attucks,
a Black man killed at the beginning
of the Revolutionary War.

About twenty thousand spectators marveled as
large groups of people marched by
silently,
protesting hatred and violence.

At the end of the march,
near Fifth Avenue and Twenty-Third Street,
James wiped the sweat from his brow.

As a man of words,
he wanted to thank everyone for coming.
But before he could say anything,
the silent marchers . . .

ERUPTED!

They had done it!
Ten thousand marchers had displayed bravery
and strength and determination.
They had shown—because of their silence—
that they would *never* remain silent when
Black people were hurt and treated unfairly.

As they all reflected
on what they had just accomplished,
every mind and heart
echoed the words
from James's famous poem.

Let our rejoicing rise
High as the listening skies,
Let it resound loud as the rolling sea.

AUTHORS' NOTE

The Silent Protest Parade, staged by the National Association for the Advancement of Colored People on July 28, 1917, was a new idea born of the terrible violence African Americans faced at the turn of the twentieth century.

Racial violence was common at the time. Lynchings, unpunished murders of Black people carried out by organized mobs, and race riots in which white residents directed bloody assaults on growing Black communities across the nation, were also increasing in number and intensity.

This increase, made worse by competition for limited resources such as jobs and housing, fueled the simmering racial tensions. This set the stage for one of the bloodiest outbreaks of racial violence, in East St. Louis, Illinois, in July 1917.

Many Southern Black people migrated to East St. Louis between 1910 and 1917. These newcomers—who had fled the harsh conditions of segregation and economic inequality in the South in hopes of better lives in the North and West—were often greeted with open hostility, especially in areas where they directly competed with whites.

The issue of jobs was front and center in the spring of 1917, when workers at the Aluminum Ore Company in East St. Louis, all of them white, staged a strike for better salaries.

Rather than meeting the strikers' demands, the company's management hired Black workers to replace the white workers.

In turn, the replaced workers erupted in anger, directing their fury not at the management but at the Black people. This led to a series of events that ultimately resulted in three days of violence, from July 1 through July 3, that left the Black community in shambles.

While the official death toll set the number at thirty-nine Black people and nine white people killed, unofficial estimates were much higher, suggesting that more than one hundred African Americans had perished in what became known as the East St. Louis Massacre.

In addition to the killings, thousands of Black residents were also left homeless because white rioters had set fire to Black homes and businesses, reducing the Black community to embers.

Like many activists, James Weldon Johnson was anxious to find a way for the NAACP to protest the massacre and other cases of racial violence.

In the past, the association had used a variety of tactics, from marches to letter-writing and direct lobbying campaigns, to demand racial justice. But Johnson recognized the need for a fresh, dramatic, and bold protest that would draw the nation's attention to the horrors of racial violence.

His proposal for a silent protest parade was welcomed by people long shocked by unspeakable assaults on Black lives. The suggestion to include children in the protest was also compelling, since young people were often the most vulnerable and the most deeply affected by the violence.

As an estimated ten thousand Black men, women, and children paraded down New York's Fifth Avenue on July 28, silently marching in step to the beat of muffled drums, their bodies bore witness to their desperate desire to see the promise of liberty and justice made real.

The signs they carried spoke as loudly as their silence. One sign shared the marchers' hope to "Make *America* Safe for Democracy." That message, with its call for the government to protect Black Americans, echoed a phrase that President Woodrow Wilson had used—to make the *world* safe for democracy—to support the United States' entry into World War I.

Other signs read, "It Is a Crime to Be Silent in the Face of Such Barbaric Acts" and "We March Because We Want Our Children to Live in a Better Land."

The Silent Protest Parade did not result in new federal laws against racial violence. But it succeeded in attracting the attention of newspapers across the country, ensuring that the East St. Louis Massacre, unlike earlier brutal massacres of Black people, would not be ignored.

Today the parade stands as an inspiring reminder of the power of protest in all forms, including silence, and the power and resilience of young people in the face of ongoing racial hatred and violence.

"Lift Every Voice and Sing"

by James Weldon Johnson

Lift every voice and sing
Till earth and heaven ring,
Ring with the harmonies of Liberty;
Let our rejoicing rise
High as the listening skies,
Let it resound loud as the rolling sea.
Sing a song full of the faith that the dark past has taught us,
Sing a song full of the hope that the present has brought us.
Facing the rising sun of our new day begun,
Let us march on till victory is won.

Stony the road we trod,
Bitter the chastening rod,
Felt in the days when hope unborn had died;
Yet with a steady beat,
Have not our weary feet
Come to the place for which our fathers sighed?
We have come over a way that with tears has been watered,
We have come, treading our path through the blood of the slaughtered,
Out from the gloomy past,
Till now we stand at last
Where the white gleam of our bright star is cast.

God of our weary years,
God of our silent tears,
Thou who hast brought us thus far on the way;
Thou who hast by Thy might
Led us into the light,
Keep us forever in the path, we pray.
Lest our feet stray from the places, our God, where we met Thee,
Lest, our hearts drunk with the wine of the world, we forget Thee;
Shadowed beneath Thy hand,
May we forever stand.
True to our God,
True to our native land.